Full Product Transparency

Cutting the Fluff Out of Sustainability

Ramon Arratia

European Sustainability Director, InterfaceFlor

First published in 2012 by Dō Sustainability

87 Lonsdale Road, Oxford OX2 7ET, UK

ISBN 978-1-909293-22-9 (eBook-ePub)
ISBN 978-1-909293-23-6 (eBook-PDF)
ISBN 978-1-909293-21-2 (Paperback)

A catalogue record for this title is available from the British Library.

At Dō Sustainability we strive to minimize our environmental impacts and carbon footprint through reducing waste, recycling and offsetting our CO_2 emissions, including those created through publication of this book. For more information on our environmental policy see **www.dosustainability.com**.

Page design and typesetting by Alison Rayner
Cover by Becky Chilcott

For further information on Dō Sustainability, visit our website: **www.dosustainability.com**

DōShorts

Dō Sustainability is the publisher of **DōShorts**: short, high-value ebooks that distil sustainability best practice and business insights for busy, results-driven professionals. Each DōShort can be read in 90 minutes.

New and forthcoming DōShorts -- stay up to date

We publish 3 to 5 new DōShorts each month. The best way to keep up to date? Sign up to our short, monthly newsletter. Go to **www.dosustainability.com/newsletter** to sign up to the Dō Newsletter. Some of our latest and forthcoming titles include:

- *Green Jujitsu: Embed Sustainability into Your Organisation* Gareth Kane
- *How to Make your Company a Recognised Sustainability Champion* Brendan May
- *Making the Most of Standards* Adrian Henriques
- *Promoting Sustainable Behaviour: A Practical Guide to What Works* Adam Corner
- *Solar Photovoltaics Business Briefing* David Thorpe
- *Sustainability in the Public Sector* Sonja Powell
- *Sustainability Reporting for SMEs* Elaine Cohen
- *Sustainable Transport Fuels Business Briefing* David Thorpe
- *The Changing Profile of Corporate Climate Change Risk* Mark Trexler & Laura Kosloff
- *The First 100 Days: Plan, Prioritise & Build a Sustainable Organisation* Anne Augustine
- *The Short Guide to SRI* Cary Krosinsky

Subscriptions

In additional to individual sales and rentals, we offer organisational subscriptions to our full collection of published and forthcoming books. To discuss a subscription for your organisation, email **veruschka@dosustainability.com**

Write for us, or suggest a DōShort

Please visit **www.dosustainability.com** for our full publishing programme. If you don't find what you need, write for us! Or Suggest a DōShort on our website. We look forward to hearing from you.

....

Abstract

IN BUSINESS, THE PAST TEN YEARS have been the decade of 'corporate responsibility'. Thousands of companies have shown unprecedented levels of interest in managing their environmental and social impacts, leading to a huge supporting industry of sustainability professionals, lorry loads of corporate reports, and a plethora of green labels and marketing claims. Ramon Arratia argues that we need to cut out all the fluff and transform this new industry and profession to focus instead on full product transparency (FPT). In the world of FPT, all companies carry out lifecycle analyses of their products and services, identifying with precision the areas where they have the biggest impacts and where they can make the greatest difference. They then disclose the full environmental impacts of their products using easily understood metrics, allowing customers to make meaningful comparisons in their purchasing decisions and providing governments with a platform to reward products and services with the lowest impacts. This book explains how a new world based on lifecycle analyses (LCAs) and environmental product declarations (EPDs) can take us away from the past decade of corporate responsibility fluff and towards a more practical era where companies make real social and environmental gains that are based on hard facts.

About The Author

 **RAMON ARRATIA** is a sustainability director with 13 years of practical experience in corporate positions at multinational companies such as Interface, Vodafone and Ericsson. He was named by *The Guardian* newspaper as one of the world's top sustainable business tweeters. He is a strong advocate of product sustainability through his popular blog (**http://www.interfacecutthefluff.com/**) and gives 50 speeches a year on the subject. He campaigns for stronger and more efficient European regulation based on product standards, for revisiting corporate sustainability reporting and for many years he led the 'Cut the Fluff' campaign against labels, certificates, partial truths, marketing claims and all the components of the old sustainability beauty contest. Ramon has an MBA from Warwick Business School, a MSC in Quality and Environment from Spain and a degree in chemistry. This mixture of business and technical education has given him a privileged perspective to understand both the geeks (LCA practitioners, academics, engineers) and the geezers (marketing, PR, sales, sustainability consultants). This book has been clearly written with a hybrid 'geekzer' mindset.

Acknowledgements

TO CONTEXT AND SALTER BAXTER that a few years ago produced the paper 'Cutting the Fluff Out of CSR'. After some years, there is still a huge amount of fluff in the industry and I recovered the line 'Cut the Fluff' for my campaign for real sustainability.

To Peter Mason who reviewed the book and translated the Spanglish draft into proper English.

To Luke Hancock who helped me on the research and initial writing of some chapters.

To Nick Bellorini from Dō Sustainability for reviewing and publishing this book.

To Jane Anderson for a thorough review of the book and her knowledge on the most technical LCA issues such as functional units.

To Dustin Benton from the Green Alliance for reviewing the book and making great points.

To Simon Propper who transformed me from a CSR cynical corporate manager to an irreverent sustainability thinker.

To Andy Raingold from the Aldersgate Group and many others who are joining me in the search for radical sustainability through product and service focus.

To all my friends at the Cambridge Sustainability Leadership Programme who allow me so often to transgress my duties and preach my ideas on FPT in their executive courses.

To PE International for leading on LCA in the corporate world, not only making LCA easy with their GaBi software but for creating a huge demand for EPDs by helping set up the German Building tool DGNB and the European 'uber-PCR' EN15804.

To my friends and colleagues Connie Hensler, Johan Wever, Agustin Lucardi and Paul Bruinenberg for teaching me so much about LCA and EPDs.

To Ray Anderson for such an outrageously ambitious vision.

Contents

CONTENTS

PART 1

The Case for Refocusing on Product (Rather than Corporate) Sustainability

1. The corporate responsibility beauty contest hasn't taken us that far

WE ARE AT LEAST TEN YEARS ALONG the corporate sustainability journey now, so what really significant changes have we achieved? Perhaps the business world has focused on the wrong tasks? Could it be that, despite all the carbon neutrality claims, hundreds of Global Reporting Initiative A+ reports and sustainability teams of ten or more people, companies have still not radically redesigned their core products and business models?

The answer is that there has been far too much focus on companies wanting to look good, and not nearly enough attention paid to actually performing well.

The beauty contest

It's in the blood of companies to compete, to strive to be better than their peers. That has been the reason for the success of corporate sustainability, because businesses like to vie with each other to be the best in this area. But the end result of all the competition has been to encourage companies to give the impression of looking good while barely changing their 'business as usual' model. It's hard to change the direction of a business, especially in the short term, but the corporate sustainability beauty contest has nonetheless been characterised by a disappointingly low level of achievement.

An entire industry has been created around this beauty contest, including thousands of labels, corporate responsibility (CR) report design agencies, boutique assurance providers, hundreds of awards with infinite categories, materiality matrix mavericks, investor questionnaires consultants, professional stakeholders looking to 'engage' with companies and all manner of membership organisations offering support networks for a hefty fee. Service-provider directories in the field typically feature more than 500 such organisations offering to help businesses look more virtuous than their peers – what the marketing guys call 'differentiation'.

The problem with all this activity is that looking more virtuous doesn't have anything to do with being more sustainable. We in the sustainability movement need to ask ourselves honestly whether we are pushing for actual change or whether we are merely helping companies to gloss over big issues by making them compete in irrelevant contests?

We offer companies the prospect of being able to make '100% natural' products or to be the first company in their sector to become 'carbon neutral'. In short, we have been tremendously innovative in coming up with fairly meaningless stuff that is easy and quick to implement, or that can deliver nice stories and marketing claims, but frighteningly ineffective at producing anything that will affect actual performance.

And astonishingly, CEOs are quite happy about their performance

A 2010 Accenture survey of global CEOs put the last nail in the coffin of CR as it stands. It found that 81% thought sustainability issues were fully embedded into the strategy and operations of their company. Yes, FULLY EMBEDDED! It's not a joke. It's actually quite sad that the most senior people don't get it.

Please someone explain to them that having a CR team reporting to public affairs with a nicely designed 150k report with some cherry-picked case studies and a set of qualitative targets plus a few quantitative targets on quick wins is not 'fully embedded'! Fully embedded means sustainability is fully taken account of in all the products of the company. You are redesigning your products, your business models, your entire value chain. Yet there is no company in the world that has achieved this. The sustainability movement should brutally tell CEOs that making wishy-washy claims such as 'Sustainability is part of our DNA' is just wrong.

Seventy-two percent of CEOs in the same survey felt the strongest motivator for taking action on sustainability issues was 'strengthening brand, trust and reputation'. Well, here we have the reason we are trapped in this rather useless beauty contest.

Prepare yourself for the next sustainability phase: Full product transparency

Somebody needs to speak out if we are to move towards something more meaningful. We need a proper comparative benchmark, so that companies can compete on what really matters – and so that the sustainability consultancy industry can sell properly useful transformative services to these companies. This book is aimed at providing this benchmark: products instead of companies.

So the next phase in sustainability has to be truly embedded by being focused on the product. We need to understand clearly the total footprint of a product throughout its lifecycle – that must be the starting point.

There has been some focus at product level but wrongly headed: Green labels

You may well be asking, 'Why does it have to be this complicated to choose the most sustainable product? Can't I just look for a product with a green label?'

It's not surprising people look for shortcuts to help them decide. After all, few of us have the time to study every purchase we make. That's why there have been so many people, from gurus, to NGOs, to certification sharks, to industry associations inventing so many lucrative labels that offer 'quick assurance' about product sustainability credentials.

But when you look carefully at how some labels are administered, you realise how flawed they are. Most are too easy to obtain, which is obvious because the easier your label is to get, the bigger your market becomes. Most labels are very narrow in scope, measuring the easiest things to measure rather than the big issues. Many lack independent certification or may even be administered by the manufacturers themselves. Many labels duplicate each other, confusing clients and obliging manufacturers to certify the same product several times. Unfortunately, some of the best marketed labels are the least robust.

Today nobody certifies whether a yoghurt or a burger is good for your health. You just get the calories and the nutrition facts and you judge. This is what this book is arguing for: the environmental impacts of products – full product transparency.

2. **It's about products, not companies!**

If you read corporate sustainability reports, you'll find that most companies still focus primarily on the environmental performance of their own operations. Yet for many businesses this focus is mismatched with their true impacts, which lie outside their operations and fall instead within the lifecycle of their products.

When you view a company in terms of the products it makes – as opposed to its offices and employees – you soon discover that the vast majority of environmental impacts occur outside its operational boundaries. In many cases the impacts associated with raw materials extraction and processing, product use and end life far outstrip any 'in-house' impacts.

Most of the impacts are outside companies' boundaries

For Interface's carpet tiles, for example, around 68% of the impact is associated with the production of raw materials, while only around 10% can be attributed to in-house operations. For companies that make energy-guzzling machines, by far the biggest impact is during the product use phase. This is counterintuitive for many people, because the most visible parts of a company's operations are either their glitzy office headquarters or their smoke-belching factories.

Sometimes the figures can be quite spectacular. For a consumer goods company such as Unilever, around 95% of a product's impacts typically come from outside the company's own operations (see figure below).

FIGURE 1. Unilever product impacts

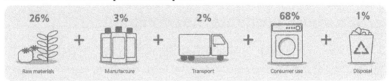

SOURCE: Unilever 2008 baseline study across 14 countries. Total in tonnes.

Tesco, a UK supermarket, says its direct carbon footprint in the UK is 2.6 million tonnes of CO_2 per year. Yet the impact of its supply chain, which makes the products that go into its shops, is 26 million tonnes of CO_2 – ten times Tesco's own footprint. And the footprint of its customers using Tesco's products is even greater: 228 million tonnes of CO_2, which is not far off 100 times the supermarket chain's own footprint.

FIGURE 2. Apple's environmental footprint

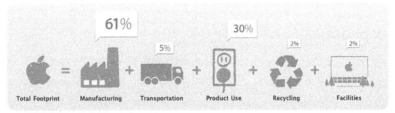

SOURCE: Apple, www.apple.com/environment

Only 2% of Apple's carbon footprint comes directly from its offices and facilities, while around 61% comes from outsourced manufacturing and raw materials, and 30% from the product when it is being used by the consumer.

The impact of 'stuff' is usually in the supply chain

When a lifecycle assessment is carried out on a physical product such as a carpet, or a t-shirt, or some ready-mixed concrete, it usually shows that the biggest impacts are in the supply chain, and are therefore already embedded in the product before they get to the company for the final manufacturing process. The biggest environmental impacts up to this point are usually associated with the types of raw materials being used, as well as the types of chemicals used to process these raw materials.

Outsourcing has made things worse

With the advent of outsourcing over the past 20 years, we now have many brands that consist essentially of a marketing department, some finance people, HR and legal units, and a product design team. The actual manufacturing of the product happens halfway across the world in nations such as China, India, Turkey or Brazil, because it's cheaper to manufacture in such places rather than in Europe or the US. This explains why so many lifecycle analyses of products show an increasing percentage of the impacts taking place outside the operations of a company.

The mismatch in management: 80% of management on direct impacts

So the bottom line is that the seemingly impressive corporate responsibility programmes and targets of many companies are in fact generally confined to minor issues, often down to the paltry level of office paper or electricity. These misinformed programmes take the attention and focus away from major issues such as raw materials use, in life product energy usage, toxic chemicals use and end of life disposal/reuse. These are the main impacts of a company that makes products, not their office lighting. The legendary green advocate Jim Fava, from Five Winds/PE International, made this crude point in a Green Mondays event in June 2011: he pointed out that 80% of sustainability management tools focus upon only 20% of the actual environmental impacts.

The key to sustainability lies in product design

The key to radical change, then, is through product design. If the impact is mainly in the raw materials, then by redesigning its products a company can use fewer raw materials, or use alternatives to them. If a product is a machine that consumes energy such as a car or a vacuum cleaner, then the key is in designing a product that is more energy efficient. And it's not just physical design that can make a difference: the business model and commercialisation strategy can have a significant influence too.

People buy products, not companies!

One of the things we need to do is to get away from comparing companies so much. After all, people buy products, not companies. It is products and services that have an impact on our lives, so that's what we should be measuring and trying to make more sustainable. Who cares whether Renault or BMW have more factories with ISO 14001, better corporate greenhouse gas reductions or have more environmental policies? We should be thinking about the impact of the cars they produce.

It's worth stating again: people buy products, not companies. We need information to decide which product is better. Buyers need that information at point of sale, and in advertisements, so that we can make an informed choice. So why are companies so busy producing corporate reports instead of product information?

Leading companies are embracing LCA as a central design strategy

Unilever is measuring the impact of all its products and brands in all countries on a 'per consumer use' basis. So 70% of its products worldwide are now analysed from this detailed perspective, with the focus being on a single serving – a portion, or the typical use of a product such as tea, ice cream, shampoo or washing detergent by the end customer. The metrics it uses are greenhouse gas per consumer use, water, packing and waste per consumer use, as well as sustainably sourced materials. You can argue whether maintaining the impact while doubling sales is ambitious enough (Unilever's sustainable living plan) but at least they are focusing on the right metrics and right scope: products.

Likewise, Boots, a pharmacy-led retailer, has developed a product sustainability assessment model that analyses 23 critical areas across the lifecycle of the product. These areas focus on the design, creation, transport, use and disposal or recycling of its products. Targets are set to drive innovation and improve the footprint per product and brand.

But still these strategies are far away from FPT

None of these examples are truly the FPT I'm about to advocate in later chapters but we can see some companies are getting closer and closer.

For example, Unilever has a target to double sales and maintain its combined product carbon footprint. Yes, it's just a factor 2 target which is not very ambitious, though they are starting to look at the right scope: full lifecycle products. Also, the Unilever target is combined product, and up to now they haven't committed to publish Environmental Product Declarations (EPDs) by each product (or product categories). The FPT that I'm advocating requires you to disclose the true, full impacts of all your products.

....

PART 2

What is Full Product Transparency and How Do You Go About It?

3. What are FPT, LCAs and EPDs?

FPT IS HAVING, AND PROVIDING, a complete picture of the total environmental impact of a product throughout its life. The emphasis here is on *environmental* impact, because the methodology for calculating this, based on a lifecycle assessment, is much more established. It is also easier to gauge environmental impacts because most of these can be measured in a quantitative way. Give us a number of years and we will be starting to integrate better quantitative metrics for social issues, most probably sector by sector.

What do we mean by each word: Full, product and transparency?

Full means full disclosure, full range of products and full scope. That means that all the environmental impacts and 'ingredients' of a product should be disclosed. That includes materials, chemicals, installation or use methods, and of course, the combined impacts on the environment, which is the bottom line. Full product lifecycle scope is about taking accountability for all the lifecycle stages of a product made or marketed by an organisation.

The 'product' means focusing on products as opposed to direct company impacts. Instead of just being accountable for the direct impacts of an organisation, note that we are talking about the product and not the corporate entity. The idea is to get the mindset shifting so that organisations not only manage their impacts but manage the impacts of their products. But by 'product' we also mean product in the wider sense, so it could be a service rather than an actual, physical item. The concept of FPT can be applied just as much to an internet search or a night in a hotel as much as to a t-shirt or a television.

Transparency means disclosing product by product, all the ingredients and chemicals, describing the methods of production, disclosing the assumptions and following international standards and product category rules.

What is lifecycle analysis?

Lifecycle analysis (LCA, also known as lifecycle assessment) is a technique to assess environmental impacts associated with all the stages of a product's life. These are:

- Raw materials, extraction, processing and transport
- Manufacturing
- Delivery and installation
- Customer use
- End of life (including impacts from disposal or recycling).

....

FIGURE 3: Stages of lifecycle analysis (LCA)

RAW MATERIALS   MANUFACTURING   TRANSPORTATION   PACKAGING   CUSTOMER USE   END OF LIFE

SOURCE: Interface, *Just the Facts Guide*

....

LCA does not consider one single environmental impact such as carbon. It considers the most significant impacts on the environment for the system studied. These are commonly measured by quantifying the impact relative to the release in kg of the most significant molecular contributor to the impact.

....

TABLE 1. Examples of categories of impacts used in LCA

Icon	Name	Description	Units of measurement
	Embodied energy – not renewable	Energy from fossil fuels	MJ
	Embodied energy – renewable	Energy from renewable sources	MJ
	Greenhouse potential	Emissions that contribute to climate change	kg CO_2 equivalent
	Acidification potential	Emissions that damage vegetation, buildings, aquatic life, and human health	kg SO_2 equivalent

Icon	Name	Description	Units of measurement
	Ozone depletion potential	Emissions that cause thinning of the earth's stratospheric ozone layer adversely affecting human health, natural resources and the environment	kg R11 equivalent
	Eutrophication potential	Emissions that increase the nutrients in water or soil affecting the natural biological balance	kg phosphate equivalent
	Photochemical ozone creation potential	Emissions of chemicals that cause smog, adversely affecting human health, ecosystems and crops	kg ethene potential
	Human toxicity potential	Emissions of materials toxic to humans, animals or plants	kg DCB equivalent

SOURCE: Interface, *Just the Facts Guide*

For more information see the European Joint Research Centre document (http://lct.jrc.ec.europa.eu/pdf-directory/ILCD Handbook Recommendations for Life Cycle Impact Assessment in the European context.pdf).

....

FIGURE 4. Example of categories of impacts in coal fired electricity generation

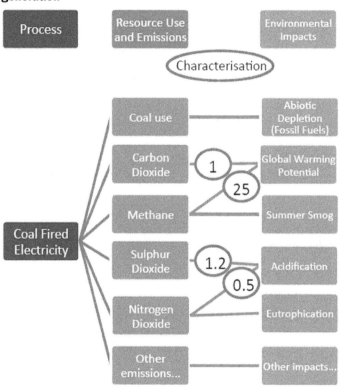

I kg of Carbon Dioxide and I kg of Methane do not cause the same amount of climate change. Methane has higher radiative forcing than CO_2 and therefore has a higher climate change impact

SOURCE: Graph courtesy of Jane Anderson, PE International.

....

LCA as a way to avoid burden shifting

The LCA approach studies whole product systems and thus enables businesses to avoid mitigating one environmental impact at the expense of aggravating another. LCAs are used because they can help avoid a narrow view of environmental concerns by compiling an inventory of relevant energy and material inputs and emissions. They evaluate the potential impacts associated with identified inputs and releases. This information can in turn help an organisation make more informed decisions. The goal of an LCA is to compare the full range of environmental effects assignable to a product or service with the aim of improving processes, supporting policy and providing a sound basis for informed decisions.

The product or service output: The functional unit

One of the key features of LCA is that it measures the impacts of a product or service instead of the direct impacts of the company that produces it. Therefore it is especially important to define the boundaries and scope related to any metric by which a product is measured. In LCA terminology this is called the 'functional unit', which defines precisely what is being studied and quantifies 'the service delivered by the product system', providing a reference to which the inputs and outputs of environmental impacts can be related.

Let's start looking at it in a very simplistic way. Think of a glass. A glass is a countable thing: one glass, two glasses, three glasses. Glasses can be counted in units. The liquid contained by a glass, on the other hand, is not counted by units but in litres. So, in a simplistic way, the functional unit needed to carry out an LCA for a glass is units, but for the liquid in the glass it is litres.

But it gets more complicated. That way you could not compare two glasses with different capacities. You would need to compare the number of glasses needed to contain a given amount of liquid, because people want the glass to drink with. You would also need to think about cleaning them. If one was crystal and needed to be hand washed, and the other could be washed in a dishwasher, then you would need to take this into account over a given number of uses. Also, if one was very fragile, typically only lasting 100 uses, whereas the other was robust, then this would also need to be included within the functional unit. For drinks, then the question is whether it is just about the volume, because you are just using them to quench your thirst, or it might be about calories. Milk needs to be refrigerated, squash doesn't.

Declared unit instead of functional unit

For most construction materials, the function cannot be finalised until we know how they will be used in the building. A carpet can provide sound proofing and thermal insulation, but this may not be required or used in the building, or may need to be compensated for if it is problematic. Cement's function can only be considered based on the concrete it is used in and how it is used. For building products, we therefore consider 'declared units' of 1 kg, 1 m^3, 1 item.

I argue that for FPT we should work on the basis of declared units rather than functional units, because a manufacturer of products should declare the impacts of their products irrespectively of how their clients will use their products. The declared unit for many raw materials, such as steel or cement, is kg. The functional unit for office space can be measured in m^2. For power generation it could be kWh. The functional unit for carpet is m^2 per product installed. That's the functional unit over which product manufacturers should strive to make impact reductions. How the products are used is a matter for customers.

This idea of focusing on declared units is likely to cause some outrage to the LCA academics but declared units can work as building blocks while traditional functional units are better for comparative studies. For example, if you have the EPD of steel and cement per kg, carpet per m^2 and so on for building materials, you can calculate the impacts of a building.

Defining functional units can get very tricky, especially in connection with services. What is the functional unit of a mobile phone service, for instance? Should it be a minute of a call? But the network is also used for the internet, so should it be MB of traffic?

For tangible things such as ice-cream, t-shirts, or pens, the functional unit is quite clear: it's what the customer gets. Unilever bases its LCAs on consumer use: one use of toothpaste, one use of rinse aid for the dishwasher, or one use of soap for a shower.

Example of functional units for LCA studies:

- Lighting 10 square metres with 3000 lux for 50,000 hours with daylight spectrum at 5600 K.

- Seating support for one person working at a computer for one year.

- 1 m² of insulation with sufficient thickness to provide a thermal resistance value of 3 m²K/W, equivalent to approximately 100 mm of insulation with a conductivity (k value) of 0.033 W/mK.

- The amount of paint necessary to cover 20 m² with an opacity of 98%.

- A single pair of dry hands (to compare hand dryers, paper and textile towels).

- 1 km of gravity sewerage system under a road in a non-aggressive soil and groundwater environment, used for the removal of mixed household water, consisting of pipes DN 300 or DN 450 and manholes DN 1200 or DN 1350, with a service life of 50 years.

Example of simpler declared units:

- 1 kg (cement, steel)

- 1 m² (carpet, office space, building)

- 1 litre (drinks)

- 1 use (toothpaste, soap)

Ancillary materials or processes

The point of ancillary materials or processes is particularly important. All the extra stuff needed to make a product or service actually work has to be taken into account. It's quite obvious that you need to take into account the fuel needed to use a car. When looking at drinks, you need to factor in whether they need to be refrigerated or heated. When looking at soap, you need to factor in the water and heating needed to use that soap.

Note that it's not the m^2 of product sold, because you need to take into account the installation waste (cutting the carpet to fit the shape of the room). You also need to factor in the impact of ancillary materials used to install it, such as underlay or adhesive.

Problems with manipulating the scope and assumptions of LCA

Lifecycle assessment alone is not sufficient proof of a positive product footprint, for the simple reason that the scope of the study can be manipulated. There have been many examples of a 'well chosen' scope that can make good features look better than they really are while making bad points virtually disappear. You may, for example, have a mobile phone made with highly toxic materials but with a good battery life that exceeds the industry average. Solution for the unscrupulous business: choose energy or carbon as your main indicator, which will hide the toxicity and emphasise the good battery life.

Some years ago we saw manufacturers of paper tissues and manufacturers of hand dryers simultaneously claiming that LCAs have shown their products had a lower impact than each other. This was because the hand dryer manufacturers assumed that customers used four paper towels per visit or a very short hot air blast, while the paper towel makers assumed one towel and a significantly longer hot air session. So it's all about fair assumptions and scope. And better if there are strong rules than just relying on the interpretation of LCA practitioners or companies.

What are product category rules and how do they fix the assumptions?

Product category rules (PCR) are a set of regulations for products in a sector or category that are established by an independent technical committee that includes experts from that sector. Each PCR has within it a set of functional units and metrics common to that industry. The rules act as guidance to help a company understand what LCA data to collect. Product category rules explain how calculations should be made and presented – so as to best capture the different elements of a product's total environmental footprint.

The PCR process is carried out in an open, transparent manner, and there is ample opportunity for various stakeholders to comment on how it is drawn up. This is crucial to making sure the PCR documents are of the highest quality possible. When all relevant comments are incorporated into the PCR it is approved and can then be used in the marketplace.

Although in theory each product is unique, it is not feasible to have a PCR for each one – that would lead to an avalanche of PCR documents. Instead, groups of product category rules have been created for similar products that consist of the same raw materials, types of chemicals, and compositions and components or for a group of different products that provide a similar function. This allows for the same set of rules to be applied to a large number of similar products – mobile phones, steaks, fridges, milk, cars, and so on.

Each PCR incorporates its own set of common functional units and metrics that are relevant to the industry in question, with agreed metrics relevant to the creation of the products or services in question.

What is an EPD?

An environmental product declaration (EPD) is a statement of a product's 'ingredients' and environmental impacts across its lifecycle. In the same way that nutritional labels help consumers compare the health benefits of food items, an EPD enables them to compare the environmental impacts of products.

Why an EPD is not just another eco-label

An EPD is not another eco-label. It is a statement of fact about the environmental impacts of a product. There are no ratings, claims or judgement calls to be made, as there are with eco-labels: an EPD itself doesn't tell you whether a product is good or bad, green or polluting; it just provides the facts to enable better informed decisions.

In the same way that a chocolate bar with a nutritional label is not necessarily any healthier than a chocolate bar without one, having an EPD does not mean a product is 'better' or more sustainable. It does, however, enable customers to compare products and choose the ones that have least impact.

EPDs give you the full picture: for example, data on several environmental impact categories. Your product might be good on global warming potential (e.g. low CO_2) but have a high acidification potential (e.g. high SO_2) and both parameters have to be reported and not cherry-picked by the company.

How are EPDs created?

The methodology used to obtain an EPD is robust, and the assumptions used in the LCA calculations behind it are standardized. This means that manufacturers cannot manipulate assumptions to favour their own product (by calculating an artificially long life-span, for example).

The methodology uses internationally recognized standards; an LCA must be conducted in accordance with ISO 14040 and the EPD must be produced in accordance with ISO 14025. All of this must be verified by an independent third party.

What does an EPD tell you?

A good EPD declaration would disclose the following:

- A list of raw materials and their origin

- A list of chemicals and their origin

- A description of raw material processing and production

- Specifications on the manufacturing of the product, including a breakdown of energy consumption and embodied energy, emissions released, treatment of waste, and packaging and transport

- Information on product use and end of life processing, including treatment of any waste and emissions released

- A table with the LCA results per impact category per lifecycle stage

- Evidence and verification for the calculations. All EPDs need to provide a report showing evidence for verification of the calculations and statements in the EPD.

Once all these data about the environmental footprint of the product have been verified by an independent third party auditor, they then need to be captured in a clear and concise declaration.

How EPDs provide full product transparency and why that matters

FPT disclosure based on EPDs empowers and enables all customers, whether they are governments, businesses or consumers, to gain a clear understanding of the total environmental and social impact of a product, including at its end of life.

Providing customers with accurate, impartial third party-certified information about the total footprint of a product allows them to vote through their purchasing decision and to buy the right sustainable product. This will not only have a positive impact on the environment and society but also on competition and innovation. It creates a clearly visible level playing field for companies offering similar products within a sector, and it forces them to compete not only on price and quality but on all aspects that go into the making of a product.

EPDs are inexpensive, contrary to the urban myth

Some people argue that EPDs are very expensive and, especially if you have too many product categories, that it becomes unmanageable. This is like arguing that Unilever or Kraft would find it impossible and very expensive to provide the nutrition facts for all their products, given their product range. Yet they manage.

EPDs are expensive if you don't do the internal work and you ask a consultant to do all the work for you. You would end up paying from

€10,000 to €15,000, which is still much less than what many companies pay for some green labels. To put this into perspective, I have seen companies in the building products sector pay more than €50,000 for various types of green labels and certification schemes of dubious independence and robustness.

Once you invest internally and a small part of your corporate social responsibility (CSR) or sustainability team have the ability to perform LCAs, it becomes very inexpensive and EPDs can be done for less than €1000, sometimes even €500. And the information collected is not only of great use externally but for internal purposes and decision-making, mostly substituting for redundant internal reporting.

TABLE 2. Example of information contained in a real EPD

Base materials / Ancillary materials

Base material	Value	Unit
PA 6	8,3	%
PES	2,9	%
PP	1,2	%
Limestone	52,6	%
Bitumen	18,4	%
$Al(OH)_3$	3,7	%
Latex	11,21	%
Glass fibre	0,8	%
Additives	0,9	%

SOURCE: Interface

FIGURE 5. Result of the LCA for Microtuft modular PA 6.6 carpet from InterfaceFlor

Categories evaluated	Unit per m²	Production	Delivery/ Installation	Use during 1 Year	End of life
Primary energy not renewable	[MJ]	162.6	2.6	3.8	-50.5
Primary energy renewable	[MJ]	7.4	$8.1 \cdot 10^{-4}$	0.3	-0.5
Greenhouse potential (GWP 100)	[kg CO2-Äqv.]	6.9	0.36	0.2	4.4
Ozone degradation potential (ODP)	[kg R11-Äqv.]	$6.5 \cdot 10^{-7}$	$-2.9 \cdot 10^{-10}$	$4.0 \cdot 10^{-8}$	$-2.6 \cdot 10^{-8}$
Acidification potential (AP)	[kg SO2-Äqv.]	$2.6 \cdot 10^{-2}$	$1.6 \cdot 10^{-3}$	$7.7 \cdot 10^{-4}$	$5.2 \cdot 10^{-3}$
Nutrification (NP)	[kg PO4-Äqv.]	$5.5 \cdot 10^{-3}$	$2.7 \cdot 10^{-4}$	$9.1 \cdot 10^{-5}$	$1.0 \cdot 10^{-3}$
Photochemical oxidant formation (POCP)	[kg Ethen-Äqv.]	$3.2 \cdot 10^{-3}$	$1.3 \cdot 10^{-4}$	$6.2 \cdot 10^{-5}$	$1.2 \cdot 10^{-4}$

The values for **the entire life cycle V_T** may be calculated as follows:

$$V_T = \text{Value}_{\text{Production}} + \text{Value}_{\text{Delivery/Installation}} + n \cdot \text{Value}_{\text{Use 1 Year}} + \text{Value}_{\text{End of life}},$$

n representing the number of years of life considered in each case.

SOURCE: Interface

4. Full product transparency at work: The magic metric that changed the car industry

What has happened to the car industry using g CO_2/km as a metric is a very good example of the depth of transformation that product transparency can deliver. This fascinating metric has enabled European regulators to mandate top-down targets for car companies, enabled customers to have a comparable reference for the car footprint and provide national and local legislators the means to tax what is higher impact and support what is lower. This transparent metric has also created competition in the car sector with the focus being upon their biggest environmental impact, 'in life use', which in turn has created a huge level of innovation in the car industry and supply chain.

A decade ago the car industry had no incentive to design cars that would consume any less petrol. It really wasn't at the core of car manufacturers' strategy. The industry used to design cars that were affordable to build but not necessarily always affordable to run. Yet according to European Union (EU) research, passenger cars make up 12% of total EU CO_2 emissions. And yet, according to the European Environmental Agency, around 77% of the impact of a passenger car is in the 'use' phase with a further 13% directly linked to the production of the fuel consumed in the 'use' phase.

FIGURE 6. Environmental impacts during the lifecycle of a car

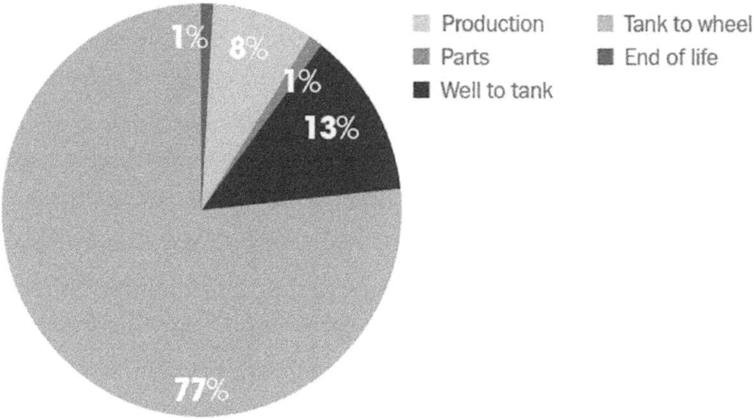

SOURCES: http://www.eea.europa.eu/data-and-maps/figures/life-cycle-analysis-of-passenger-cars and http://ec.europa.eu/environment/ipp/pdf/jrc_report.pdf

For this transformational change to take place an overall regulatory framework at EU, national and local level was needed. Furthermore, and crucially, a common industry metric was required that could be used in the car industry. That magic metric was to be tail-pipe (exhaust) emissions measured as grams of CO_2 per kilometre driven (g CO_2/km).

Although incomplete, because it didn't take into account whole-life CO_2 emissions and environmental impacts, this partial transparency at least focused on the biggest issue and has transformed the industry. g CO_2/km has given a purpose to policy-making, often bureaucratic, expensive, ineffective and siloed. Below is an overview of some of the key regulatory interventions this common standardized metric has enabled.

First, the bottom-up approach. The EU Car Labelling directive was enacted to ensure that a label on fuel economy and CO_2 emissions is attached to a car or displayed in a clearly visible manner near each new passenger car model at the point of sale. This bottom-up approach was based on driving transparent competition, which in turn enabled the customer to make an informed decision taking into account the biggest environmental impact of the product. Most customers might still choose a car mainly by the design or the brand but at least they have the right to know the impact of their decisions. What has been the main result of this transparency? It has cut off all the 'greenwash'. No manufacturer today is doing green marketing on the little things they are doing in their factories or their recyclable seats. Why? Because this wonderful metric is allowing customers to say, 'please cut the fluff and just tell me the g CO_2/km for this car'. Sustainability commoditized as it should be, like money: terrible news for marketing agencies, great news for the world.

The beauty of such a metric goes beyond 'point of sale' to 'all promotional materials'. Thanks to the same directive, today all car advertising must include the g CO_2/km for that specific car being advertised. That has created consistency and transparency whilst simultaneously empowering the customer to not only become accustomed to the metric but make critical buying decisions based on this metric. My mother today knows that 160 g CO_2/km is too much and 100 g CO_2/km is acceptable. Many Londoners know cars under 100 g CO_2/km don't pay the congestion charge. Consistent transparency creates customer literacy and awareness which leads to change.

Second, the old-school, top-down approach. This key metric allowed an EU-wide regulation that came into law in 2009, requiring each manufacturer to decrease their average portfolio of emissions to 130 g CO_2/km by 2015 and 95 g CO_2/km by 2020. In 2008, the average g CO_2/km for car emissions in the UK was 158.0 g CO_2/km. In 2009 that figure was 149.5 g CO_2/km so the change because of legislation is huge. Look at how effective those ugly technocrats from Brussels have been! How ironic that the UK Climate Change Committee highlights cars as one of the few successes of carbon reductions in the UK.

This legislation came about because the EU ran out of patience with industry voluntary agreements. Yes, those voluntary agreements so loved by politicians because they don't have to impose any difficult decisions. In 1998, the European Automobile Manufacturers' Association (ACEA), JAMA, and KAMA agreed to reduce average CO_2 emissions from new cars sold to 140 g/km by 2008. That was a 25% reduction, quite considerable. But predictably when there is no stick or carrot on the table, the car manufacturers' commitment achieved a mere 2.2% reduction between 1998 and 2006. What would you expect? So the EU set up a mandatory target and crucially gave a sensible period of time (2020) to allow companies to invest, innovate and so make the necessary widespread changes required to meet the targets of this regulatory framework. It also came with sticks in the form of financial penalties. Surprise, surprise, it's working! CO_2 emissions from new passenger cars have started decreasing substantially: 1.6% in 2007, 3.2% in 2008 and 5.4% in 2009. That's the beauty of the market: tell it what you want to achieve and it will find a way to do it. The problem is that on many occasions we don't tell the market, our supplier, what we want, or worse, we don't have the metrics.

These two combined policies, of setting agreed, clearly measurable targets and making this information clearly visible to the end customer are completely changing the playing field of competition within the car industry. And this competition through innovation will compel manufactures to meet the EU-wide target of 95 g CO_2/km by 2020. Car manufacturers are doing what they are best at – designing cars – as opposed to inventing labels, patronising customers with green marketing, 'engaging' employees, sustainability reporting and other semi-useless stuff.

But our beloved metric goes much further. It can transform national and local policy-making aimed at changing behaviours and purchasing decisions. One example at national level is the French Bonus/Malus scheme. Simply put, customers choosing to buy a heavy polluting car will pay extra tax on the price of the car, whereas customers choosing to buy a more fuel efficient car will receive a reduction in the price of the car. The tax penalty ranges from €200–2600 per car. The incentive reductions range from €200 to €5000 and higher for even cleaner cars. Around 31% of new vehicles will be eligible for the bonus, 25% for the malus. There are around 44% of new vehicles currently emitting between 130 and 160 g CO_2/km that are not affected by the new measure. Furthermore, the bonus will be deducted from the price paid to the dealer and must be identified and visible on the bill. These facts will also provide incentives to dealers to sell cleaner cars.

Another example is UK company cars. In the UK you pay more tax for your company car if your car produces more CO_2. For example, for a car of less than 75 g CO_2/km the tax rate for petrol cars is 5%. For a car of 150 g it is 19% and for a car of 235 g it is 35%. This is a good example of variable tax on a clean or dirty product. The more you pollute the more tax you pay.

But our magic metric is also very useful at the local level. In London, cars which emit 100 g/km or less of CO_2 and meet the Euro 5 standard for air quality qualify for zero congestion charge. A 100% exemption from congestion charge also applies to electric vehicles. In many towns in the UK such as York, Salford or Milton Keynes and Richmond, one can have discounted residents' parking if you have a low carbon vehicle and free parking if you have an electric car.

Guess what? Customers are paying attention to the environment! Such a crazy bunch of tree-huggers...

....

FIGURE 7. Average CO$_2$ emissions of new passenger cars in Europe (g/km)

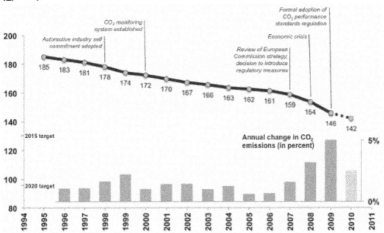

SOURCE: European Commission

....

There is more to it. Once a common metric is mandated, comparable data are obtained. And when data are available, people invent great ways to communicate and compare the data. Non-Government Organisations (NGOs), car magazines, think-tanks and other civil society actors collectively are far more creative at explaining the data to the customer than a bunch of bureaucrats in a room designing an 'official' label. A new area of work has begun in making sense of the magic metric data to help the customer buy the right clean product.

Let's look at some of the examples:

- Nextgreencar.com offers a full rating based on the environmental impact of each car and includes for each car g CO$_2$/km: **http://www.nextgreencar.com/search_database/index.php**

- The UK government (DVLA) offers a page where you enter your registration number and it tells you the g CO_2/km of your car: http://www.taxdisc.direct.gov.uk/EvlPortalApp/

- Many magazines and websites such as carpages.co.uk/CO_2 have a car browsing function based on their CO_2 emissions and have ratings of cars according to their emissions: **http://www. carpages.co.uk/CO2/**

- Other websites offer advice and a calculator for your company car tax such as comcar: **http://www.comcar.co.uk/**

- Coolestcar have as their sole purpose to advise customers on choosing the car with the lowest impact: **http://www.coolestcar. co.uk**

And when data are available, people make decisions based on proper data (even better if the environmental decision is rewarded with lower taxes). There are an interesting bunch of buyers very likely to make purchasing decisions based on cold facts rather than on impulse: corporate and public buyers. An example is the case of Essex County Council, with a fleet of 850 vehicles, 74% of which are cars. This local council outsourced their fleet in 2008 on a buy-and-lease-back contract. At the same time they set an emissions cap of 160 g CO_2/km for any new delivery and their average today is 135 g CO_2/km.

But you don't have to own a fleet to be the key decision influencer. Ask the sales people at Interface in France. By 2008 they could only choose a car with less than 140 g CO_2/km – so no more gas-guzzlers allowed. Likewise Arval, part of the BNP Paribas Group, have a fleet averaging 128g CO_2/km after it refreshed its own company car choice list for employees to include a wider variety of the lowest emitting vehicles on the market.

Many companies, governments and local councils are amplifying governmental policies on car tail-pipe emissions just because there is a magic metric that allows them to make a quick decision.

5. How to revolutionise other industry sectors through a magic metric: A practical guide for policy-makers

So how do we get beyond the car sector? Below is a brief guide to creating transformational change within a sector or product category based on the concept of FPT.

1. Do an LCA in order to understand the main environmental impact of that sector or product category (e.g. food, buildings, chemicals, electricity, etc.).

2. Develop a common metric based on the full lifecycle impact or at least on the main impact area.

3. Establish a long-term goal stating what performance is required by when. This can be a fixed value or variable in order to increase competition.

4. Establish minimum performance required and ban underperforming products (you might get some World Trade Organization issues but there are always ways around it).

5. Create a system where industries pay penalties for underachieving and/or tax credits for overachieving. That encourages industries to compete and innovate.

6. Mandate visibility of the common metric on all promotional materials.

7. Enable and encourage national taxes, whereby the products with more environmental impact pay more and products with less impact pay less (variable product tax).

8. Enable local regulation that gives 'incentives' to products with less impact (e.g. what free parking and free congestion charge is doing for the cars).

9. Support and enable data intermediaries to be creative and do their job to help consumers make sense of the data.

10. Release the power of public procurement and buy only products that achieve certain performance levels.

11. Encourage equally the power of corporate procurement.

12. Award with the EU Ecolabel those products that demonstrate more than 50% impact reductions over the average product.

13. Sit and relax – the market usually delivers (but you need to tell the market what you want).

Let's look at the building sector and try to apply this thinking (in a very simplistic way):

a) Magic metrics could be kWh/m^2 and kg of embodied CO_2/m^2 (I will focus on the first one).

b) Set up a minimum European standard of, let's say, 100 kWh/m^2 for new buildings in 2020.

c) Give the EU Ecolabel to new buildings under, let's say, 50 kWh/m^2.

d) Give tax discounts to new buildings under, let's say, 50 kWh/m^2.

e) Facilitate licences/permits to the super-performing buildings (e.g. fast track or no permit required).

f) Existing houses pay variable rate of stamp duty and local council tax according to their energy rating (would encourage retrofit more radically than green deal type of approaches).

g) Government would commit to the strongest standard for new buildings and would retrofit existing government buildings to a minimum standard.

h) Mandatory energy ratings displayed in every public and private building including offices, retail, etc.

This is a back of the envelope approach that does not take into account the fine details such as the differences in building types such as domestic, office or retail, but it gives an idea of what the magic metric approach can deliver.

6. Guide for companies to truly embed sustainability at the core: how this seemingly naïve idea of full product transparency can align companies and their value chains

FPT has the power to align the stars – to create a consistent approach to sustainability activity in every part of the business and to get everyone telling the same story. It allows you to get to the point where your product designers focus on the same thing that your sales force talks about, where what you say to your suppliers is the same as what you say to your customers, and what you report to stakeholders is the same as your marketing claims. The facts generated from the lifecycle assessment form the basis of all information communicated, which means that everyone sings from the same hymn sheet.

Sustainability is not part of a company's DNA until it is embedded in its products

Many CEOs claim that sustainability is part of their company's DNA. What a cliché, what an easy thing to say, impossible to prove or dispute. But how can sustainability be in a company's DNA until the core product or service of the company has significantly less impact? The real DNA of companies are their products or services, what they offer to customers, what they sell. The first thing is to understand the true impact of your products.

Product sustainability questions get you to that elephant in the room

Interface discovered that around 70% of the overall environmental impacts of their carpet tiles were related to the raw materials used to make them. Of these, the oil-based nylon yarn, just one single raw material, had the single biggest environmental impact. In fact, nylon production accounts for almost half of the impacts across the full lifecycle of a carpet tile, a hard pill to swallow for a carpet manufacturer (the fibre is what makes carpet a carpet).

Rather than neglecting the elephant in the room, Interface re-focused its efforts where it could make the biggest difference: reducing the amount of yarn used, finding ways to recycle old yarn into new, and looking for bio-based alternatives to nylon. Today the company has products made out of 100% recycled nylon using half the amount of yarn, cutting the overall environmental impact by half. As a side note, some other carpet manufacturers were marketing wool carpet as a natural and sustainable option but wool has between four and six times more embodied carbon than virgin nylon.

Non-product sustainability strategies don't face the elephant in the room

If companies don't start with product sustainability, with a proper LCA, they focus primarily on reducing the impact of their own operations without realising they are missing the biggest impacts in the supply chain and through customer use. Let's look at some examples.

Banks, oil companies, lawyers and consultants are the best investors in green buildings. But hello! The main impact of a bank is not its building energy use but to whom it lends. Oil companies should do the LCA not only of their product (oil, fuel for cars) but the LCA at transportation scope level, which would give them elephants in the room to identify. Lawyers and consultants should be transparent about who they work with and the ethical standards of their products and services.

After you do an LCA or ask profound questions about your core product or service, then you must be prepared for the unexpected – and be ready to change your strategy as a result, no matter how inconvenient it may seem.

Aligning the stars

The magic of embracing FPT is that it provides a consistent focus for everyone involved in every part of the business – from product designers and innovators to marketing, sales and procurement staff. Here's how it works:

Designers forced to redesign

The first thing that happens when you identify the key impacts of your product is that you have to redesign the product to reduce those impacts. This immediately gives your designers a clear objective, focusing on reducing key impacts rather than 'feel-good' green gimmicks. Committing to performing a lifecycle assessment, whether it's light or full, for every new product before it is launched gives your designers strong signals about what the company wants from them. How can a designer produce a more sustainable product without knowing what 'more sustainable' is? Without the information provided by an LCA, brainstorming sessions come up with concepts such as 'locally produced', 'natural' ingredients, or a product made with the use of wind power. As a result, time and money is channelled into product redesigns that sound bold and innovative, but actually make very little difference to the overall impact of a product. By contrast, the results of a lifecycle assessment give design teams the opportunity to say 'OK, we now know that 80% of the impact is in this area, so we need to work on reducing that impact'. It's a no-brainer.

Supply chain management without the 700-question questionnaire

The second thing that happens after an LCA is that the product managers should tell their purchasing colleagues to translate the findings of the LCA into requirements for suppliers. For example, once Interface knew that its biggest impacts came from virgin nylon yarn, it asked its suppliers to come up with a way to radically increase the recycled content in the yarn. One of the suppliers saw this big opportunity and invested in a re-polymerisation plant to meet this demand and is now delivering 100% recycled yarn made from old nylon fishing nets.

FPT using information from the LCA enables a company to set out clear expectations to its suppliers and to focus on the activity that matters. It means a company can ask its suppliers to come up with radical, practical innovations that will significantly reduce the environmental impacts of the product, rather than tinker around the edges. Supply chain management becomes less complicated, too. Instead of sending suppliers 700-question questionnaires with inane requests such as 'do you have an environmental policy?' or 'have you signed up to the Global Compact?', you can cut to the chase and talk to them directly about how they can help you to reduce the impact of your product. How transformative is a box-ticking questionnaire compared with asking suppliers to respond directly to your biggest environmental challenge?

Marketing with a ready-made angle instead of inventing labels

Once your suppliers have helped your innovation colleagues to produce more sustainable products, this enables your marketing department to make environmental claims based on fact, not greenwash. The marketers now have a ready-made 'angle' for the product, as they are promoting something that has genuinely been designed to be sustainable. They no longer have to come up with post-justifications about the product's sustainability. Like everyone else in the company, the marketing team can focus on communicating the big impacts that really matter. They have no need to come up with another green label or gimmick, as the message is embedded in the product itself.

Promotion materials with full transparency leave little scope for sales reps to exaggerate

By the same token, your sales staff can now enter LCA facts into their tender documents and sales materials. FPT means a customer can clearly see the impacts of a product across the various stages of its production and use, so this enables a comparison of your product with others. Printing this information on marketing materials means the sales force has no scope for sexing-up stories; the facts are right there in front of everyone, and cannot be altered. What is more re-assuring: if I tell you to trust me, that all my company's products are good for the environment, or if I tell you: 'this product has 5.7 kg CO_2 and this one has 12.9 kg CO_2'? In the latter case, you have the hard facts – along with the other usual information about as design, price or service. You can use all of these facts to make a buying decision.

Customers enabled by the pure facts

Let's forget consumers for a moment. My mother in the supermarket does not really care about the amount of kg CO_2 in the products she buys. She doesn't have the time or the inclination to look at the facts. But there are other customers who do, including:

- governments that have committed to public procurement but don't know how to make buying decisions because the product providers can't give them the information they need, so at the moment they are relying on labels

- B2B (business-to-business) buyers, such as architects, who design green buildings but are unclear as to which products to use

- retailers such as Walmart or Tesco who are driving carbon emissions reductions across their supply chain but have very little data from their suppliers to work on.

With these customers, and others, the demand for plain facts as opposed to catchy labels or stretched claims is out there right now – and it's growing. This is the interesting bit about the stars aligning; when customers also align to FPT thinking, then things begin to happen. And if your company is tuned into that customer demand for transparency, then you are delivering yourself a huge competitive advantage.

Getting everyone into line

If companies were mandated to publish FPT information, then they could hardly just ignore the information that this brings forth. As a consequence most of them would begin to reduce the impact of their products almost immediately. They would be forced to set targets, show progress and benchmark themselves against competitor's products. This is what happened with sustainability reporting. Now we need to take this competition to the more fertile product territory.

If this brave new world were to emerge, then retailers would be able to edit the choice of products they offer to consumers, and they could nudge suppliers to improve the impact of their products. Perhaps only 5% of consumers would care about sustainability, but under these circumstances, that would be enough to change things.

The alignment would not stop there. Governments would have full knowledge of product impacts and could enact all kinds of policy instruments based on that information. NGOs would have the full data too, so they could focus on some bad product categories and apply pressure for improvements to be made. Government procurement teams could also then support the growth of environmental products by making fully informed decisions to buy the most sustainable products and services.

7. How full product transparency will revitalise the bureaucratic approach to managing sustainability in the supply chain

The conventional approach to exercising corporate responsibility in a company's supply chain is to draft a company supplier standard and then audit for compliance using that document. The process often begins with a questionnaire and is followed by audit visits to suppliers judged to be the highest risk. The better programmes also include an offer of 'capacity building' for suppliers – in other words, they provide training and support to help them raise and maintain their standards.

Positive and usually well-intentioned as this course of action is, the impact is inherently limited by the narrow scope of the dialogue and the teacher–student nature of the relationship. It might work well when addressing very problematic issues (such as child labour), but telling suppliers what they shouldn't be doing misses an opportunity to foster their talent for commercial advantage and innovation.

The flaws of the 700-question supply chain questionnaire

The questions below are from a real example of a supplier questionnaire I was asked to fill in by a corporate customer. Let's look at how little each question actually drives real environmental performance:

1. Does your organisation have an environmental policy in place?

Any company can write up a policy in a couple of hours, but this doesn't mean the policy is being implemented or monitored. Policies by themselves don't drive performance, so the creation of an environmental policy will not necessarily have any impact on the products you are buying from your suppliers. For non-sophisticated audiences, it looks so good to say that 80% of your suppliers have an environmental policy. But in reality it means next to nothing.

2. Does your organisation have an environmental management system (EMS) in place?

ISO 14001 and EMAS are management systems, not performance systems. They just require an organisation to have a policy, comply with legislation, determine its impacts, and have targets. There is no link with performance. The other issue is the scope of these management systems. In general, they have a purely internal focus – they don't include the raw materials used to make products, nor do they look at the use phase impacts of those products. If your suppliers have an EMS in place, this provides little assurance that the products they are supplying have less impact on the environment than any others.

3. **Has your organisation identified the specific environmental impacts associated with the products, services or works it provides and taken steps to minimise them?**

   The supplier can just answer 'Yes, we have identified them'. But how do you know that the issues it has identified are the biggest and most important ones? The supplier can also respond with any amount of corporate spin – cherry-picking some initiatives from the fringes and thereby allowing itself to look good.

4. **Does your organisation observe legislation with regards to environmental issues?**

   Shouldn't this be taken for granted?

5. **Does your organisation communicate its environmental policy to its suppliers?**

   What demonstrable impact can be gained from sending a piece of paper full of generalities to suppliers? It would be far better to ask suppliers for radical innovations on the issues you want to improve.

6. **Does your organisation check the environmental policy and performance of its staff?**

   Even if your supplier does this, how much of a difference will it have on the products you are buying?

The ideal questions for suppliers

The ideal questions for suppliers should concern the performance of the products you are buying from them. After all, you are not buying the whole company. Besides, most of the impacts occur most likely outside company boundaries.

The problem with developing the right questions is that it depends on the product you are buying, so unfortunately it's just not possible to copy and paste from one company to another. This is probably bad news for lazy consultants.

But it's not that difficult. First, you need to understand what the biggest issues are for the products you are buying. Are they in the raw materials, like a carpet, or are they in the use phase, like a car? Then it becomes a matter of understanding the key environmental indicators that can measure these impacts, combined with the right functional unit such as kg CO_2/km, kWh/m^2, embodied water/kg of product, etc. If you are buying products with toxicity risks, you should ask for the list of materials and chemicals used – and their quantities. Perhaps you shouldn't concern yourself with this because the EU has done the work for you with the REACH (Registration, Evaluation, Authorisation and Restriction of Chemicals) regulation.

All of this assumes that you have an understanding of the impacts of the products you are buying, which is paramount to making a difference. If you don't, you can still ask some general questions but stay more focused at product level. For example, this question works for most products: can you prove through a third-party peer reviewed LCA or an EPD that your product is more environmentally friendly than that of your competitors?

8. If you sell to the government, you'd better understand full product transparency: How Green Public Procurement is becoming based on transparent metrics

The real demand for sustainability is coming from B2B and public procurement

There are three key buying powers in the world today: governments, corporates and citizens. Both government and corporate procurement teams are now making big buying decisions through tendering processes, based not just on price but also on the environmental and social facts surrounding a particular product or service. The problem today is that there is little or no transparency on the real social and environmental impacts of products and services, so buyers from government and the corporate world have to invest vast amounts of time and money developing lengthy and time-consuming sustainability questionnaires. Often the focus of these is less on relevant aspects of the product or service and more on labels and certificates, which are pounced upon as some kind of proxy environmental assurance. FPT, however, will enable public and B2B procurers to make informed choices based on real facts, while saving lots of time and money on the wasteful bureaucracy that is connected with form-filling.

Public procurement is a huge market and it's a willing one

According to the European Commission white paper, *Public Procurement for a Better Environment* each year European public authorities spend up to 16% of the European Union's Gross Domestic Product on products and services such as buildings, transport, cleaning services and food. This amounts to approximately 2 trillion euros annually. That is massive by anyone's standards. Imagine the transformational power that could be brought into being if this buying power was used to favour goods and services with lower impacts on the environment. Through their procurement policies, governments could make a significant contribution to the speedy development of a market for sustainable goods. As we have seen previously in the car industry, new legislation can change the rules of the game dramatically, and regulation to introduce sustainability into government procurement would certainly do that. That's why Green Public Procurement (GPP) has been adopted and targets set in 21 member states.

Here are some EU figures. CO_2 emissions would be cut by 15 million tonnes per year if the whole of the European Union adopted the same environmental criteria for lighting and electronic equipment as the city of Turku in Finland, where citizens have reduced electricity consumption by 50%. If the European public sector alone were to adopt the Danish Ministry of the Environment's guidelines for cars, CO_2 emissions would be cut by around 100,000 tonnes per year and fuel and operating costs by a third. But if all cars operating in Europe met these standards, then CO_2 emissions would be reduced by 220 million tonnes, contributing significantly to the EU greenhouse gas emissions reduction target for 2020. This is an example of a simple yet very powerful and wide reaching action that could immediately reduce our negative impact on the planet by dramatically reducing emissions and pollution.

But how can anyone buy green if they have no clue on how to choose?

Imagine you are the person making public procurement decisions in a local council or a university. You are more than willing to buy green, and are being encouraged by your superiors to do so. But none of the suppliers are giving you full transparency on the environmental impacts of the products you would like to buy. They are all providing you with biased information, funny labels and some half-truths.

Perhaps the EU has some guidance? But you discover how little help the EU offers. All you can find are vague phrases saying that procurement teams should 'take into account energy consumption and emissions' or that they should consult the TC/CEN 350 standard – or that they should follow the self-serving advice of choosing products with an EU Ecolabel. Wouldn't it be easier for the EU just to say something like 'choose cars with less than 120g CO_2/km'? Everybody understands that metric, all manufacturers now provide it, and it's an easy piece of advice on which to base decisions.

That's the beauty of FPT. It helps people to make decisions based on easily understandable magic metrics rather than requiring purchasers to have PhDs in environmental science in order to buy a piece of furniture for the office.

Green public procurement should not be based on labels, narrow criteria and urban myths

The old way was to link public procurement to eco-labels, which is just unhelpful because it shifts decisions about what is green on to third-party private intermediaries, some of whom are certification sharks. Private labels are made to earn money and tend to lower their standards so as to get as many clients on board as quickly as possible. Furthermore, the popularity of such labels has more to do with clever marketing than actual performance-based environmental criteria.

Government-owned labels are not much better. In the EU, green public procurement documents suggest the following as an example of good practice: 'By 2015 all cleaning services should use products meeting the EU Ecolabel criteria.' However, are technocrats in Brussels the best people to design good criteria for cleaning products? When you look at the current EU Ecolabels, you can see the fingerprints of the lobbyists all over them. For example, the European Ecolabel for flooring products was developed in Italy, and it's therefore no surprise that the criteria are more favourable to ceramic flooring (where Italy is strong) than for carpets (a more Northern European-focused industry).

Other targets are not much better. At first sight the EU sets a seemingly commendable one for schools, saying that '50% of meals served in school canteens should be organic by 2013'. But is organic really a key issue for the food industry? What about land use, soil protection, loss of biodiversity and water use? Sometimes certain targets – such as this one – appear to be created purely because they are easy to measure and certify. Doing the real work on discovering the true impacts of products and services is far more difficult than setting a binary target.

Green public procurement based on process certifications is even worse

Public procurement based on process certifications such as ISO 14001 is even worse. ISO 14001 only guarantees that you have a process for complying with legislation, coupled with a process to deliver continuous improvement on that position. It does not set performance criteria or outputs. It does not guarantee any environmental product performance. The main focus is upon the organisation and how it operates, not on the products it offers – how they are designed, how they perform, and how they are disposed of or reused. Yet ISO 14001 is used all over the place by public procurers because they lack product-related magic metrics and they have to rely on something. In desperation, ISO 14001 is an easy lifebelt to hold on to. The Estonian Environment Ministry, for instance, tendered for cleaning services in 2010 and included the following in its technical environmental specifications:

- cleaning services to be delivered in accordance with ISO14001 or equivalent

- all plastic bags must be biodegradable

- waste shall be sorted (packaging, organic waste, etc.)

- toilet paper and hand towels shall be made from recycled paper

The funny thing is that this tendering process is presented by the EU green public procurement handbook as an example of good practice. But it's not. Rather than looking at the biggest impacts of cleaning products – such as the toxic chemicals used within them – the ministry has rushed in to gather together a set of criteria that are easy to find and implement. The result: a set of useless touch-points that fail to address the bigger issues. Estonia's criteria make no mention of the use of chemicals, or of energy efficiency, or of cleaning equipment. If you create green criteria using brainstorming sessions of unqualified civil servants rather than impartial product specialists – and if you fail to take account of FPT – then this is what will happen.

Magic metrics are a better way forward in the medium term

The use of magic metrics is a far more effective way to develop decision-making and buying criteria. We don't need guidance, labels and handbooks. We need metrics that are specifically related to the products and services that are being bought – metrics that can be used by all countries, that encourage transparency, foster competition on sustainability, stimulate innovation, and offer a simple framework for making important buying decisions. In a magic metrics approach it's much more difficult for an industry lobby to defend their position than tinkering with qualitative criteria and exceptions. Transparent metrics also reassure the consumers and buyers at all levels. With eco-labels, you are asking consumers to trust the label, with metrics you are empowering them to make a decision based on facts instead of patronising statements. The car industry has shown that this can work, so just think what it could be like in other areas. Imagine the change that could be brought about if we had a world where:

- a local council specifies that it will only use taxis that operate on less than 120 g CO/km

- a government department looking for new offices specifies that it will only consider buildings with energy requirements that result in less than 20 kwh/m^2 for heating and cooling needs

- hospitals purchase all food with an average water footprint per kg of food under 400 litres and all the meat purchased below 100 litres

- a government department such as the Foreign Office chooses a preferred airline based on kg CO_2/passenger/mile

- a university states that it will only buy cleaning products that are free of certain chemicals

- a defence ministry stipulates that it will only buy trucks based on performance on kg CO_2 per tonne-km and NOx emissions.

These scenarios are easy to achieve, and not that expensive to arrive at. We just need to make the decision to go there now.

....

PART 3

How Full Product Transparency will Revolutionise Business Relations with Consumers, Investors, Policy-Makers and Society

9. Consumers might not care that much but full product transparency can still stimulate real demand for sustainable products

AFTER MANY YEARS OF WORKING HARD to encourage consumers to change their buying habits in favour of sustainable products, we have seen only small pockets of success.

Let's face it: Not many consumers are really prepared to bother

Unfortunately, although there is growing public awareness of the urgent environmental matters we now face, only a small section of the consumer market is changing its buying behaviour. According to research performed by Marks and Spencer (M&S), the UK consumer market contains a 'deep green' group of consumers representing 8% of the market, as well as a 'lighter green' group representing 28%. Aside from these two factions, there is a segment of consumers (38%) who could be persuaded to buy green if the price, quality and convenience of a product is good enough. And then there is a recalcitrant hard core (26%) who do not really care about sustainability issues and are unlikely to change their buying behaviours in any circumstances.

Furthermore, many research projects have suggested that even among those consumers who might be inclined to think about sustainability issues, only a small percentage will make purchasing decisions based on the environmental information displayed on a product label or on the web. It's hardly surprising that most consumers don't have the time or the inclination to search out detailed environmental information when they are making minor purchases of, say, a toothbrush or a cauliflower. Would you really bother to look at environmental information for the 200 items of the weekly shopping cart?

Voluntary sustainability penalises the consumers who do bother

The problem with this kind of 'voluntary sustainability' is that it actually penalises the people who bother to make the right purchasing decisions – mainly because it asks them, in most cases, to pay more, let alone endure the hassle of going through all the information. After a while, even deep green consumers begin to question why they should be taking the hit by buying more expensive stuff when, elsewhere down the supermarket aisle, someone who doesn't care about the environment is being rewarded with a cheaper shopping basket.

What, they ask themselves, is the point of making such sacrifices, and why should they act more or less on their own? These are fair questions, and there is no easy answer to them. Those who make the right choices should not be penalised. So what we actually need is a new system that moves away from voluntary sustainability and makes good behaviour a viable and rewarding option for everyone. We must look at other ways of instigating the wholesale change that we need.

The right to know: same story as for the 'made in X'

A better way for the environmental movement to leverage the power of the consumer is to adopt the 'right to know' approach. Rather than working under the false premise that consumers must self-flagellate themselves into buying sustainable products at a higher price than other goods, we should appeal to their basic right to know what is in their products. This can be a far more transformative strategy.

Today it is standard practice in many product labels to see 'made in x'. Who really makes a decision to buy a t-shirt by looking at whether the t-shirt is made in Thailand, China or Turkey? Not many, I suspect, but still transparency is required. More useful information is provided on nutrition facts for food and specifying the textile fibre a cloth is made of. Not everybody will look at it, let alone make a decision based on it, but it's transparency and it's a customer right. You don't argue against a customer right.

Under the UK Sale of Goods Act of 1979, for instance, the customer has a right to know what is in the product that he or she buys, and, among other things, whether the product is 'of satisfactory quality' and is 'fit for purpose'. It is only a short step to show the consumer whether the product has been created using sustainable, renewable raw materials or with clean energy. The use by large corporations of raw materials such as palm oil, soya and other crops from unsustainable sources in thousands of products has led to a growth in interest in this area from consumers and NGOs alike. So it now falls on businesses to meet and exceed these growing expectations by proving that their products are sustainable throughout the entire value chain.

The power of going through the transparency process

All of this can be achieved partly through product labelling (think of a car or a washing machine), but it's not only the product label itself that matters, it is the process that companies must go through to provide such information as well as the third-party validation that proves the data are right. Collecting LCA information focuses a company's attention on how to reduce the negative impacts of their products. For many companies, it's actually quite revealing and they realise where the real impacts are. Also, it spurs them into further product innovation in terms of redesign, sourcing and manufacturing. Third-party validation encourages the type of thorough analysis and procedure that consumers and governments expect business to go through to prove their products are sustainable.

I expect companies bother for me

As most consumers don't have time the time or inclination to think too much about buying sustainably – and are rarely willing to pay much more for sustainable products – there is an increasing expectation that brands and companies must do the 'heavy lifting' themselves. As David Bent from

Forum for the Future has pointed out, companies used to hide behind their customers by saying, 'We're only selling what they ask for'. But there are now a number of retailers that are beginning to take responsibility for setting standards. The approach taken at Boots, for instance, is that instead of bothering its customers about sustainability, it will just get on with reducing the impacts of its products so that its customers will automatically be buying a better product for the environment whether they want to or not.

Boots is not the only company that has adopted this 'choice editing' approach. In January 2008, B&Q, the UK's largest home improvement retailer, made an important decision to stop selling its popular patio heater once current stock had run out. The Energy Saving Trust had estimated that a propane patio heater with a heat output of 12.5 kW produced around 34.9 kg of CO_2 before the fuel ran out after approximately 13 hours. This is equivalent to the energy required to produce around 5200 cups of tea. At the time B&Q was the largest seller of patio heaters in the UK, and it was appalled by the statistics. So the company's management simply decided to stop selling the heaters – mirroring similar commitments from smaller retailers such as Notcutts and Wyevale. ASDA's consumer research shows that their customers want to be choice edited to avoid bad environmental impacts: **http://your.asda.com/system/dragonfly/ production/2011/12/15/16_13_37_444_Green_is_Normal_ASDA_ SustainabilityStudy.pdf**

The environmental movement needs to force retailers to take responsibility for all the impacts of the products they sell. The easiest way is through EPDs.

Edit the choice of the small day-to-day things because I don't have the time

Moves such as this by B&Q take the emphasis away from the consumer having to make purchasing decisions and towards allowing the customer to trust the retailer to deal with the biggest environmental impacts in its products. That's how it should be, with sustainability as the norm and the most unsustainable products withdrawn from sale.

If retailers edit out the choice of unsustainable products, then consumers won't have to worry about what choices they make in the future. In the final analysis, customers would much rather not to have to worry where a product comes from, what is in it, and ultimately, whether it is sustainable. As consumers we just want to enjoy buying and consuming the product, and to leave it at that. After all, if companies are making the effort to facilitate sales through great customer service, guarantees and home delivery, wouldn't they also make the effort for environmental decision-making?

Consumers largely buy on impulse on a day-to-day basis, especially for the smaller things. You see something, you want it, you buy it. Corporate buyers purchase in bulk, they make decisions based on facts. They know very well prices and how the supply chain works, and they understand the technical specifications of products. These are the people for whom an EPD will make sense – rather than my mother in the supermarket.

I will bother though for a few big items such as a car or a house

The consumer makes certain decisions less on impulse and more on a rational basis. When we buy a big item such as a car or a house that is either very expensive or will affect our lives over the longer term, then we tend to make a more thoughtful decision. In that case, we have an opportunity to take into account the sustainability parameters of what we are buying, especially if 'more sustainable' is cheaper in the longer run. For example, today many car and house buyers care about energy consumption, the durability of the product, and the cost of maintenance – or even, sometimes, how the product will be affected by future environmental legislation, such as vehicle congestion charges or requirements for energy efficiency ratings for homes.

Just tell me in a simple way what is the issue and what I have to do

There are, however, instances where the major impact of a product is not related to the buying decision, but to how the product is used. In these circumstances, the company (either product manufacturer or retailer) can better fulfil its responsibilities by trying to influence consumer behaviour.

For example, both Proctor & Gamble and Unilever have discovered – thanks to lifecycle assessments – that a large element of the environmental footprint of their clothes washing products is down to the energy needed to heat the water to wash the clothes. Both businesses have therefore now designed washing powders that can wash clothes at 30 degrees Celsius. Through visible product labelling and advertising, they have asked the customer to change the setting on their washing machine to 30 degrees, telling them that this will save them money and reduce their environmental impact. Retailers such as Marks and Spencer have added labels into their clothes recommending washing them at 30 degrees, and washing machine manufacturers have produced machines with 30 degree programmes, so reinforcing this message. Consumers now understand the benefits and have begun to change their behaviour.

Now, what would be more re-assuring? That society rely on these consumer goods companies doing these initiatives on their own, based solely on their will to be a better company? Or that on top of that, there is a system that forces those companies to take responsibilities for the full lifecycle impact of their products and publish the progress product by product line?

10. How full transparency can make policy instruments more effective

Policy-makers could benefit greatly from strategic use of the concept of FPT. Environmental information from EPDs can be used as a basis for economic instruments such as taxes and rebates, performance standards, eco-labels, voluntary agreements and public procurement. FPT can lend a very strategic intent to an array of existing policy instruments by aligning them to common goals, strategies, and visions.

Voluntary agreements usually don't work

For a whole industry sector to approve a voluntary agreement, it will usually have to be set at the level of lowest common denominator. This is due to the fact that the industry laggards don't want to risk losing any competitive advantage. For example, manufacturers of less energy efficient equipment will not accept the idea of putting in place a very high energy performance standard that takes them out of the market or places them at a disadvantage. That's why the more ambitious performance standards are usually those that come directly from policy-makers rather than from the industry.

The industry lobby groups, on the other hand, are set up to protect the status quo and avoid change, so might be less open to these innovations. That is why voluntary agreements often head for something like the 10–20% mark on reductions, compared with the 60–80% that is needed.

The problem with legislative controls

Legislative controls such as compulsory standards, permits or bans appear to be straightforward as they deal head-on with an issue. But they have many problems. Bureaucracy is one of these. Obtaining a permit (such as to expand a factory line) can eat up time, as well as staff resources and consulting fees. There is often a lot of fuss involved: calling the local authorities, drafting and drawing plans in the right format to the authorities' liking, applying for the permit, waiting for the results of consultations with neighbours, and booking a date for officials to appear on-site.

Another problem with legislation is that the rules we really need are often politically unpalatable. Most politicians have shied away from imposing punitive taxes on air travel, for example, as they know such a move would be unpopular with a large swathe of the population.

And the most important one is that legislation enforcement is very expensive.

Subsidies

Subsidies can help a new industry to hold its own in the early stages of its development. But usually they are extremely expensive and don't offer good value for money. There might be instances when they are critical though for bringing in new technologies. WWF's **Picking the Winners** report elaborates on this point.

Economic instruments: Shift the tax burden

The answer to these problems is quite simple. What we need to do is shift the tax burden onto product pollution and away from jobs, incomes and profits. Such a shift would not increase the overall rate of tax at the national level; it would simply mean that everyone – businesses and people – pay different amounts of tax according to the way they behave. This would move things on to a 'pay as you burn, not pay as you earn' footing, and so would reduce the tax burden on many people's income. This follows the 'polluter pays' principle: low pollution households and businesses will see their tax bill fall, while high polluting households and businesses will see their tax bill rise.

The concept of FPT in this context argues that highly polluting products and services should attract far more taxation by way of a variable product tax than those cleaner products that are not polluting. EPDs enable policy-makers to see fully transparent data about the real impacts of products – such as their embodied energy, the use-phase impacts, and the transport miles involved – and therefore to introduce taxes on this basis. There are many advantages in looking at environmental taxes through this product and service perspective.

Economic instruments work better with FPT

Taxes, fees or exemptions are fairer when they are applied to comparable things such as products with the same functional unit (a tomato with a tomato, a TV with a TV). They can be fairer due to the fact that they compare products that are the same instead of applying the same rate of tax to different products. It's also fairer because it can be revenue neutral, for example the lower performance can subsidise the higher performance and the balance can be neutral, which helps politically.

Full transparency can also raise the possibility of taxing actual impacts on the environment, as expressed by magic metrics such as kg CO_2, kg SO_2 or kg PH4. Eco-taxes are examples of Pigovian taxes, which are applied to a market activity that generates negative consequences for society. What could be a better form of Pigovian tax than directly taxing the real environmental impacts of products as identified through FPT?

So FPT helps governments to tax the right thing, rather than to introduce taxes based on political motivation. Basing taxation on the information available from FPT makes policy more technical and less politicised.

11. Full product transparency: The future of reporting

Good corporate reporting is based on the principles of accountability and transparency. When reporting on sustainability, this transparency is greatest when focused at product level. After a decade of corporate responsibility (CR), FPT heralds a new era for reporting. With many – and often most – environmental impacts occurring outside a company's boundaries, extending reporting from the narrow confines of a company's own operations to the wider effects of the products it sells demonstrates superior accountability. This is the ultimate in transparency. It is also of greater relevance to most stakeholders, who are more interested in a company's products than its facilities.

Accountability across the whole value chain

So forget reporting at company level. Classic CR reporting is too narrow in focus, and it misses too much. Environment sections of reports are usually limited to the immediate impacts of a company's operations, perhaps with a nod to managing impacts in the supply chain. By extending reporting to include the impacts of products throughout their lifecycle, companies can demonstrate transparency and accountability across the value chain.

A supermarket should take accountability for the products that go through it, not just its buildings

Which environmental impacts, for instance, should a retailer be account-able for – and report on? The environmental impact of a supermarket extends well beyond the doors of its stores to include the impacts of all the products it sells. These occur before and after the products enter and leave the stores – in their production, their use and their disposal. Yet conventional corporate reporting would largely ignore anything that happens outside of the store, apart from a few cherry-picked case studies.

By taking accountability for the impacts of products across their lifecycle, retailers can gain a much better idea of their overall impact on society – and of the type of products they might want to sell. Arguably, it was this kind of approach that led the do-it-yourself retailer B&Q to stop selling patio heaters. A traditional CR approach would not have registered the significant environmental impacts of patio heaters in their use phase. Ikea is now assessing its products based on a sustainability product scorecard to assess the lifecycle impacts of its products, including waste, energy and water from their use in customers' homes.

A traditional corporate report might pick out one or two products as case studies and look at their impacts, but what about the rest? If a company produces EPDs based on lifecycle assessment for all its products, this can reveal its overall impact much better than any CR report. An EPD takes into account the ingredients of a product, the methods of its production, and the full environmental impact of each stage of its lifecycle.

If we apply the supermarket approach to other sectors, we can see a different level of debate about who should be accountable for what. What about a private equity firm owning various companies? Rather than ticking some boxes and sending back a meaningless Stanford Research Institute-type questionnaire, private equity firms could report the overall impact of each of their companies based on the products these companies sell or make. This would be possible if those companies all produced EPDs for their products. The same thinking would apply to project finance.

Double counting is OK

The lifecycle approach to reporting does, however, raise the issue of double counting. Reporting has been dominated by accountants, and environmental reporting has therefore been developed along financial reporting lines. Company A owns 33% of company B so it must account only for 33% of the environmental impacts of company B. Does this really work?

For the accountancy profession, accuracy is paramount. In financial terms, double counting is a disaster to be avoided. But for environmental reporting, does it really matter? After all, the aim is to identify and cut environmental impacts globally. It's better to over-report these impacts than to miss some out. If they aren't reported by anyone, they're not being addressed by anyone. In this case, double counting simply means that impacts are being tackled on more than one front – by the supplier, the retailer and the end-user. That has to be a good thing. Yes, there might be instances such as in regulatory reporting linked to taxes where double counting might not work, but from the point of view of companies' accountability, it is a good thing.

The example of washing clothes at 30 degrees is a good example of 'triple counting', where three types of product manufacturers (M&S clothes, Unilever detergent, washing machine manufacturers) could share the benefits of reduced consumption.

Customers don't read CR reports

CR reports can be useful for sustainability wonks and some NGOs. But most customers don't read CR reports. Both consumers and business-to-consumer (B2C) customers are not interested in the company; they're interested in its products they buy. They want to know about the environmental impacts of the products they are buying, such as how much carbon, toxicity or recycled content they have, and publishing an EPD provides that information in a validated way.

However, an EPD can be quite a technical document that few people will understand. But you don't communicate the actual certificate, you communicate data. For example, one way to make this information digestible is to use a magic metric that neatly summarises the impacts. This puts the information in customers' hands to help them choose a more sustainable product. If you are buying company cars, you no longer have to worry about how many ISO 14001 compliant factories BMW has, or what kind of score it has registered with the Carbon Disclosure Project. You simply look at the g CO_2/km metric for the cars you're buying.

Investors also look at the product's data in the end

There are two main attitudes to CR reports from the sustainability investor analysts: those who throw away all the CR reports that they receive and those who do all the work and pass it to the fund managers who throw it away later on. For both types of investors, in the end they make sustainability-related decisions on other sources of information.

Investors need to understand a company's future cash flows, which derive from the ability to sell products. To understand sustainability risks and to see the actual impacts of the products provides more insight into the fortunes of a business than the generalities and corporate spin of a company report. You need to do an analysis of the risks product line by product line since risks and opportunities are different.

In the car industry, for example, investors need to have a handle on the tail-pipe emissions from each vehicle to ensure that the company will still be able to meet impending regulations, or if it will be able to compete with other manufacturers that are rapidly reducing their emissions. Data-rich EPDs can provide more user-friendly information for investors, who are data focused, than narrative CR reports. Investors aren't pushing for EPDs yet because EPDs are still a geeky subject, but once they become more readily available, they will understand their full quantitative potential and EPDs could become a cornerstone of environmental investment assessments. Give them a few years...

The best assurance is full transparency

Expensive external assurance of CR reports is used by companies as a way to verify what they're saying. But many stakeholders find the resulting bland, heavily caveated statements unsatisfactory. FPT eliminates the need for this type of assurance, which would be a relief to everyone but the self-maintaining assurers industry. Product reporting is the ultimate in transparency – clearly showing the environmental impacts of each product. By building third-party assurance into the EPD process at product level, for instance by auditing the data that goes into the EPDs, the classic CR report assurance statement becomes redundant.

What could be more reassuring than a company making a promise to cut the impacts of its products, and then annually publishing its EPDs to show whether those impacts are reducing or not? Certainly not the standard boilerplate assurance statement at the back of a CR report.

Imagine this example. You suspect your wife is cheating on you. She comes back with a certificate from her lawyer, who states that he 'has no reason to believe that your wife is cheating' and a few caveats in small print. On the other hand, your wife provides you with a fully itemised mobile phone bill. Which one would you trust more? Certificate or transparency?

....

For Product Safety Concerns and Information please contact our EU
representative GPSR@taylorandfrancis.com
Taylor & Francis Verlag GmbH, Kaufingerstraße 24, 80331 München, Germany

www.ingramcontent.com/pod-product-compliance
Ingram Content Group UK Ltd.
Pitfield, Milton Keynes, MK11 3LW, UK
UKHW040928180425
457613UK00011B/290